Riding
from Scratch

Riding
from Scratch

THE ADULT
BEGINNER'S HANDBOOK

Josephine Haworth

St. Martin's Press
New York

Copyright © 1979 by
Josephine Haworth
All rights reserved.
For information, write:
St. Martin's Press, Inc.
175 Fifth Ave., New York, N.Y. 10010
Manufactured in the United States of America

Library of Congress Cataloging in Publication Data

Haworth, Josephine.
 Riding from scratch.

 1. Horsemanship. I. Title.
SF309.H39   798.2'3   80–442
ISBN 0–312–68230–1

Contents

Acknowledgement

I would like to express my gratitude to Angela Whatman, B.H.S.A.I., for all the help she has given me in the preparation of this book.

Introduction

Everyone knows about horses:

1. Horses like sugar lumps.
2. If you walk behind a horse it kicks you.
3. You pull the left rein to go left and the right rein to go right.
4. You kick them to make them start.
5. You pull hard on the reins and shout 'Whoa' to make them stop.

Easy.

It is a pity that horses do not understand these elementary facts.

When you try to ride them they just can't get anything right. You say the proper things like 'hup' and 'walk on' and you bash your heels against them until your calves sting, but they won't move.

When they do get started they go their own way without consulting you. If they break into a trot it means they have passed the half-way point of the ride and are anxious to return to the stable where the company is better.

They may canter. It's not your idea – probably something they ate.

When you pull hard on the reins to stop them they just pull back even harder and keep going.

It is no fun at all being at the mercy of one of those jolting, head-strong brutes.

More people are riding horses for pleasure all the time. If they are telling the truth and they really do get pleasure out of it, maybe there is more to riding than is immediately apparent.

Riding ought to be impossible. People are the wrong shape for it and horses are so much bigger and stronger than human beings that the idea of anyone being able to control a horse is absurd.

To make matters worse, horses can think. They can make up their own minds about what they are going to do and there is no guarantee that it is what you want to do. Somehow, you have to get a horse to cooperate with you.

The trouble is that expert horsemen and horsewomen make it look too easy. The art of good horsemanship is to make riding appear effortless and elegant, so that is what they do, and it confuses people.

You feel a fool if you say you can't ride, but you are likely to feel even more of a fool if you pretend you can ride when you can't.

The solution is to take lessons. If you can swallow your pride and admit that you need to start from the beginning, you have the chance to become a really good rider – a much better rider than the people who have muddled their way through without proper instruction.

You will be given a horse who knows how to behave itself with beginners and then, step by step, you will be taught to do things as they should be done and that means that you will be riding not only well, but safely.

There is no truth in the saying that 'you have to fall off before you can call yourself a rider'. That is a myth put about by a lot of irresponsible people with broken collar bones.

You can fall off later on if you want to – when you are good enough to take a calculated risk with a horse or with a jump that you know is difficult.

The first problem is to find somebody good enough to teach you, because only the best will do.

You can get a list of local riding schools from the classified section of the telephone book; but after that you should go and look at the stables for yourself, and, if possible, watch a lesson. Although everything starts from the same fundamental groundwork, different schools cater for people with different aims. Try to decide whether you just want to learn enough to enjoy a quiet ride or whether you are aiming higher – towards dressage, eventing or show jumping – and make sure to choose the right school for your needs.

Find out if the people with the right qualifications for teaching are actually giving the lessons. If the only people you can find all appear to be under the age of sixteen, run for your life.

Look at the horses: are they well-cared for, healthy looking and are they behaving themselves?

Look at the stables: are they clean? Cleanliness is next to good horsemanship too.

Look at the riders: are they wearing hard hats and sensible boots or shoes? If they are not, the people in charge are not as safety-conscious as they ought to be.

Look at the saddles and bridles on the horses: are they clean and in good condition or are they held together with bits of string; and, as far as you can tell, do they fit properly?

If you decide you like the look of the place, talk to one of the instructors and tell them honestly how much or how little you know. Don't lie because they will know whether you have been telling the truth or not in the first three minutes of your lesson.

Then all you have to do is to book yourself a lesson and leave the rest to them.

If possible try to arrange to have short lessons at frequent intervals at first. For a beginner a long lesson can be a waste of time and money because your muscles will get tired out before the end.

Do not ask how many lessons you will need before you can ride. They cannot answer that question. It depends on the individual rider. The prices for lessons vary throughout the country and from one school to another, but are roughly from $15 to

$25 an hour for a private lesson and from $8 to $12 an hour for a group lesson. You can usually book just half an hour if you would prefer, especially for an individual lesson. Having the instructor all to yourself in a private lesson means that you will progress faster, but unless you are in a great hurry to learn to ride you will probably find that group lessons will suit you very well. Hacking (which means going outside the school for a walk, trot and a canter with a group of other riders) costs about $5 to $10 an hour; but a good school will not let you hack until they are sure that you can control the horse reasonably well and walk, trot and canter without falling off.

Nobody will expect you to know what every part of the horse and every part of the tack (saddle and bridle) are called when you go for your first lesson, but if you become infuriated by people constantly using technical terms that you do not understand, here they are for future reference:

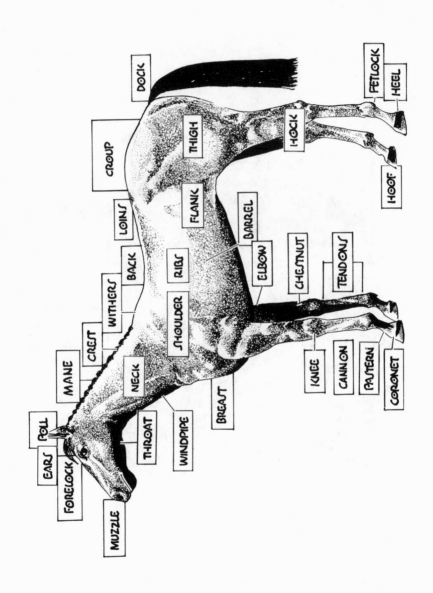

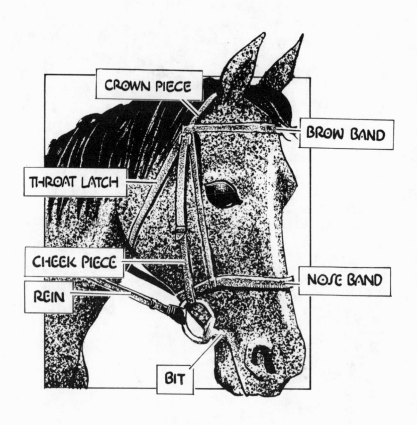

CROWN PIECE

BROW BAND

THROAT LATCH

CHEEK PIECE

NOSE BAND

REIN

BIT

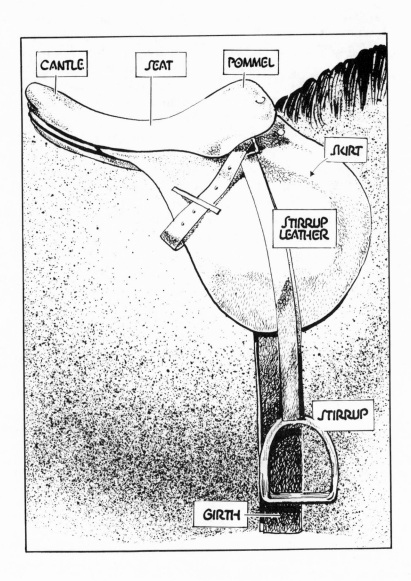

WHAT TO WEAR

A riding hat is absolutely essential. You may be able to hire one from the stables, so ask about that when you book your lesson. You may be able to borrow one, but you must be sure it is a good fit. (When you try on a riding hat, hit the brim with your hand and if it comes down and bangs you on the nose, the hat does not fit you properly.) If you are really stuck and need to buy a hat, look in the Yellow Pages under 'Horse' or 'Saddlers'. A riding hat will cost you about $20 to $25.

Trousers or jeans are perfectly acceptable for riding as long as they are roomy enough to allow you to sit astride the horse. Jodhpurs give you more protection – you do not get so many rubs or bruises on your legs, but they cost up to $40 for adults.

The school will expect you to wear sensible boots or shoes for riding – by which they mean boots or shoes with a hard sole and with a low heel. Shoes without a heel are dangerous because there is nothing to stop your foot from slipping right through the stirrup. Buckles are dangerous because they can catch in the stirrups when you want to get your foot out.

ONE

The First Lesson

You arrive at the stables for your first lesson wearing your hard hat and feeling like a fool.

They bring out the biggest horse you have ever seen in your life. That is your horse, you understand. The one you are going to ride. Dear God!

They quickly explain what the various parts of the animal are called, but it is difficult to concentrate because you are too busy marvelling at the sheer size of the thing. And then they tell you that this is a pony. This is a PONY?

The first thing they teach you is how to get on. *Mounting*. They get you to stand on the left side of the horse and the instructor leaps on and off several times to show you how easy it is. It doesn't look easy at all. Just watching drains all the strength out of your legs so that you have difficulty standing up.

Now it is your turn. 'JUMP UP,' they say.

After a lot of bother you finally get your toe in the stirrup, grab the saddle, which is somewhere above your head, and start hauling yourself up. It is rather like rock climbing except there aren't enough toe and hand holds.

When you have hauled up far enough to be standing on the stirrup, you give an almighty swing and get your right leg over the horse's back. You land face down on its neck, the instructor pushes you back into the saddle, and you are on. What a height!

The instructor says that it was not good enough. 'GET OFF AND DO IT AGAIN.'

You scramble off and wonder what to do next. It is no good letting the stirrup down to a reasonable height when the instructor is not looking – I've tried that – it just means that it is impossible to get your right leg over the horse's back.

The only thing seems to be to try it exactly the way they told you in the first place. Which is: stand on the left-hand side of the horse, by its neck. Take hold of the reins with your left hand above the horse's withers (the withers are just in front of the saddle), face the horse's tail, then pull the far side of the stirrup towards you with your right hand and get your left toe in. (It is much easier to lift your foot up high enough when you are standing sideways to the horse instead of facing the saddle.) Having got your left toe into the stirrup, point it downwards so that you don't kick the horse and then hop round on your right foot until you are at right-angles to the horse with your knee against the saddle. Put your right hand on the middle of the saddle and then give another great big hop so that you spring up into the air and, as you spring, swing your right leg over the horse all in one movement.

It works. How remarkable. While you are congratulating yourself, the instructor is pointing out that you are not supposed to land in the saddle with a bump because horses don't like it.

Sorry, horse.

Never mind, you're on. (Later, when you are mounting on your own, be sure to hold both reins firmly with the offside (right) rein slightly shorter. This means that if the horse starts walking forward it is going to move away from you and not tread on your toe.)

You're mounted. Right, what's next?

Now comes the most important part of the first lesson. The instructor will *put* you into the 'correct' riding position. First you must sit with your seat tucked underneath you, not bulging out behind. Keep the bottom of your spine straight, back

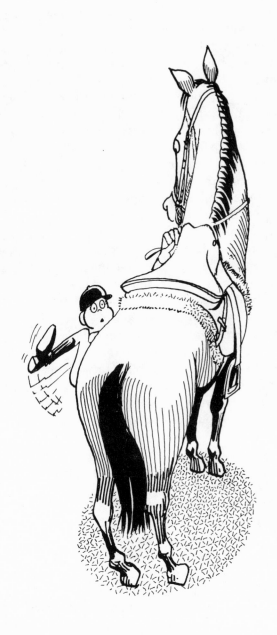

relaxed, shoulders back and down, head up and chin in.

That is your body taken care of.

Now your legs: the instructor will take each of your legs in turn, pull them back and down and turn them inwards, so that the insides of your thighs are against the saddle – the *insides* remember, not the backs. Your knees should be slightly bent and your feet directly underneath you with your heels down and your toes pointing forwards. It's not easy.

This will be the first time you have been asked to keep your heels down when you are riding a horse, but it will not be the last. It is important because when you push down with your heels the muscles all the way down the inside of your legs come into action. They may have been unused for years, but now you need them.

The instructor will probably suggest that you push your toes down to see what happens. What happens is that those muscles disappear; you can't feel anything; you have no contact against the horse. So it's heels down, heels down all the time.

When you are sitting in position on the horse you should try to get your pelvic bones (remember your pelvic bones?) to widen out as much as possible so that you can get deep down into the saddle. You should be sitting between two straight lines – one running down from your hands to your knee, to your toe; and the other from your ear to your shoulder to your hip to your heel. When you look down, you should just not be able to see your toes.

It feels perfectly awful when you first try it.

The reason why they put you into such an uncomfortable position on a horse is to stop you losing your balance. Take away the horse and you will see what they mean. If you stood on the floor in the 'correct riding position' you would not fall over because your feet, body and head are all in a straight line. You do see people sitting on horseback in an armchair position – with their legs stuck out in front of them – try it on the floor and you will fall over backwards. Some people lean forward when they ride. If you stand on the floor and lean forward more than a

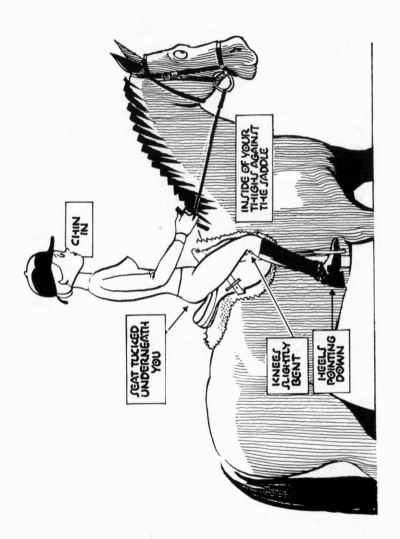

few inches you fall forward. The same applies on a horse. You have to be balanced so that you will not fall over, *because on a horse you don't fall over, you fall off.*

Up to now the horse has been standing still, but the instructor suggests a walk round the yard. Why not?

As a beginner, you will almost certainly be told to LEAVE THE REINS ALONE.

While they lead the horse round for you, don't just admire the view (which is always interesting from the back of a horse), but concentrate on your position. It may not be all that comfortable but when the horse is moving it does seem to work rather well.

Your instructor is leading you gently towards the fundamental truth about riding horses. Your hands and legs are not going to keep you on. When you are riding correctly, you have other things to do with them. Real horsemanship means being able to stay on through balance, suppleness and feel alone. That far-off dream is called 'the independent seat'.

As you stroll round the stable yard, get used to the feeling of the horse moving underneath you. Follow the movements by trying to relax and let your hips move with the horse – four beats to the bar.

The insides of your thighs, flat against the saddle, should be steadying you as the horse moves, steadying – not gripping.

'Everything all right?' says the instructor. I should say so. You have only been on the horse for ten minutes, but somehow it *feels* right. Quite different from those shaky little outings in the past. The most memorable thing about them was a feeling of acute anxiety.

If you are not sure of yourself, nature works against you, making things worse. If you are anxious, it makes you stiff – clenched from top to toe – and rigid, so that you bounce about on top of the horse like a stick of rock, which is both unnerving and uncomfortable. Unfortunately, the body's natural reflexes to fright are usually the worst things you can do when you are riding. A moment of alarm and you find yourself bringing your knees up towards your body. It is just as natural a reflex as taking your hand away from something hot. But on horseback bringing your knees up pushes you to the back of the saddle and upsets your balance. Perched up there you are much more likely to fall off. You have to be ready for that natural reaction and when it comes, reverse it. What you should do if you are feeling unsteady is to push your legs down. The more leg you have in contact with the horse the safer you are going to be – which is obvious when you think about it.

The great advantage of taking lessons is that you know you will be riding a horse which has probably been ridden by hundreds of beginners before you. There is nothing to worry about. Relax and concentrate on your lesson.

What about trying a trot? The instructor explains that she would like you to do a 'sitting trot'. That means that you sit down in the saddle while the horse trots.

Splendid. Have a quick check on your position and you are ready.

The instructor says that you may find it a little bumpy at first, but try not to bounce.

Fine, let's go.

'TROT ON.'

The instructor and the horse trot. The horse is now travelling at about six miles an hour and feels like a de-railed train. Every time one of its front feet hits the ground you bounce up into the air and come down again with a bang. If you were a pint of milk you would be turning into butter.

After a while the instructor stops. She looks disappointed. 'You're bouncing,' she says. 'I told you – you're not supposed to bounce.'

It is difficult to reason with someone when you have no breath.

'Now try it again, and relax,' she says. 'You've tensed up.'

I wonder how that happened!

'Right. TROT ON.'

The most pressing problem is that all this bouncing is

23

making your nose run and what are you supposed to do about that?

Just a minute, though, something truly dreadful is happening. No balance at all, wobbling about all over the place. Help!

The instructor looks back. 'GET YOUR HEELS DOWN. PUSH! PRETEND YOU ARE TRYING TO REACH THE GROUND.'

That's better.

A bit more bouncing and you stop for a rest.

The instructor explains that we are now going to try 'the rising trot'. The idea is to rise in the saddle so that you miss every other bump. That sounds like a good idea.

She explains that as you rise you should incline your shoulders slightly forward so that the line of your body runs parallel to your lower leg. Keep the small of your back straight and your seat tucked underneath you. Bring your hips forward and up so that your weight is over your thighs and knees.

What?

Keep the movement as small as possible. Don't push yourself up, let the horse do that. It's UP, DOWN, UP, DOWN.

Right? TROT ON.

'UP, DOWN, UP, DOWN,' the instructor shouts helpfully as the horse trots. 'UP, DOWN, UP, DOWN.'

But it turns out to be more like 'UP, DOWN, DOWN' in your case. The instructor stops and explains that up, down, down is wrong. You had a feeling it might be.

Some people get the knack of the rising trot very quickly. Some take longer. It's a landmark. 'Do you trot?' they asked when I first got in touch with the stables. 'Not intentionally,' I said.

If you do find it difficult, it is a good idea to hang on to the neck strap if your horse is wearing one. That makes you feel steadier and also ensures that as you rise you will be pulling yourself slightly forward. You can grab the horse's mane to get the same effect if you want to – if the horse is used to beginners he won't mind.

The better you are at the rising trot the more restrained the movement will be. Springing up and down like a ping pong ball is a sure sign of a bad rider. It probably means that someone somewhere has allowed him to stand on his stirrups and push himself up. He might think that he is rising to the trot, but all he is really doing is a lot of standing up and sitting down.

The great advantage of trying the rising trot during the first lesson is that by the time you have finished struggling to get it right you are exhausted. When the instructor tells you that you are now going back to the sitting trot it's a great relief. Nothing to do but sit there. So you sit there doing nothing –

and –

MY GOD, YOU'VE GOT IT!

You're jogging along in perfect rhythm with the horse. Not a single bounce. It's so easy. It's wonderful and it's poetry. Horse and rider in perfect harmony.

Has the instructor noticed?

Has anybody noticed?

Look, look, I'm riding!

The instructor looks back. 'That's good,' she says, smiling at you.

You are smiling too, smiling like some sort of an idiot, all over your face. You could keep this up for hours. It's wonderful.

The instructor stops. The horse stops.

'I hope you have enjoyed your lesson,' the instructor says, rather formally.

Oh no, it's all over. Just as you had got the hang of it. What a tragedy.

Dismount. Getting off is much easier than getting on because you can see where you are going. *Both* feet out of the stirrups, lean forward, hands on the withers, swing your right leg over the horse's back and slide down to the ground. Don't play silly beggars and pop your right leg over the horse's head. It could be very dangerous if the horse raised its head or moved suddenly.

By some trick of the light, when you get off, the horse you

have been riding looks much smaller than it did when you first saw it.

'How big is it?'

'Fourteen hands.'

'Is that good?'

At the end of your first lesson you rush off exhilarated (and legless) to book for another one. Nothing is going to stop you now. Just wait till you tell everyone about that sitting trot. What a triumph. When's the next Olympics?

Since every riding school varies, you may not find your first lesson corresponds exactly to the one described here, but whatever happens, the next day you will feel stiff.

Exercises help. It is rather boring to think that you have to start doing physical jerks at home, and of course you don't have to, but if you want to get your muscles and joints to supple up more quickly there are a few simple exercises you can do that will make a noticeable difference:

Ankles: For the beginner, ankles tend to be the stiffest joint and with stiff ankles you can't get your heels down. During your first lesson you will have had to push down as hard as you can but you don't want to have to push – you want that joint relaxed so that your heels come down naturally. Supple your ankles up by (a) lifting one foot off the ground and rotating it for as long as you like; (b) stand on a step or the bar of a gate – get just your toes on the step, hold on to something and then alternately stand on tiptoe and lower yourself until your heels are as low as they will go.

Wrists: Shake your hands up and down as fast as you can until your wrists are completely relaxed. If you shake them for long enough your hands will feel light – almost floating. When you take up the reins (later on) that is how your hands should feel to the horse – light.

Legs and Hips: Standing on the ground, swing one leg as far forward as you can, down again. Now straight out to the side and down again. Then kick out behind you and down again. Keep doing this with one leg and then the other. (This exercise won't do your back any harm either.)

Any sort of suppling exercise will help – shrugging your shoulders up, back and down; touching your toes, swinging your arms round and round in circles.

These exercises are all optional, but you will also, during the course of your lessons, be expected to do some exercises while you are on horseback. These usually involve things like arm-swinging, touching your toes, leaning right back until you are lying on the horse and getting up again (very good for the stomach muscles) and a little exercise called 'going round the world' which means turning yourself right round in the saddle by moving one leg at a time. If you honestly feel that you're not up to 'going round the world', say so. But most people can manage it, even if they prefer to do it with someone holding on to the horse and with another helper standing by them if necessary.

All the leg exercises are designed to help you open up your hip joints because then you can sit deeper in the saddle, and the deeper you sit in the saddle the safer you will be.

Doing exercises on horseback not only helps the riders to supple up, it also gives them confidence. When you have been swinging round in the saddle, touching your horse's ears and tail, lying on its back and going round the world, riding round the school in a normal position seems quite easy.

TWO

Push Not Pull - The Aids

It is all very well having someone to lead the horse round for you or to give you a lesson on the lunge (that means that you ride round in circles while someone stands in the centre holding the horse on a long lead – the lunge. It gives you the chance to learn a great deal in a short time because you have the undivided attention of your instructor and you are not concerned with the problems of controlling the horse.) But one day you are going to have to manage the horse by yourself. And to get the horse to do what you want it to do you are going to have to communicate with it.

All the methods used for communication between rider and horse are known as 'the aids'. It is interesting that they are called aids rather than commands, but understanding that distinction is central to understanding what riding is all about. Because a horse is a living creature with a mind of its own, you can't just issue a series of orders and expect them to be carried out automatically.

The whole point of the aids is that not only do the signals you give with your back, seat, legs and hands let the horse know what you want him to do, but they actually help the horse to do it.

Once you understand the aids and how to use them you stop being a passenger and become a working partner with your horse. *It is only the combined efforts of horse and rider that can produce results.*

Of course all the aids are designed to work together, but let's start with the back, seat and legs.

Suppose you are sitting on your horse in the stable yard and for the first time there is no one holding it for you. You are all by yourself, in charge, with the reins in your hands and your feet in the stirrups.

(The stirrups should be at about the level of your ankle bone if your legs were hanging straight down. They are for auxiliary balance only – say at canter or on the turn – and at first they are nothing but a nuisance because your feet keep slipping out of them. The stirrup iron should be across the ball of your foot. The only way to make it stay there is to keep your heels down all the time – you get distracted for a minute, and you've lost your stirrup.)

You have the reins in your hands. Passing between the third and little fingers, through your hands and over the first fingers, held in place firmly with your thumbs on top. The reins should not be slack but taut enough for you to be able to feel the contact with the horse's mouth. Just keep that contact, keep it light and DON'T PULL. We will come back to the reins later.

You are in position, you are balanced and you are ready to go. Your idea is to walk the horse out of the stable yard and into the school for a lesson.

Good. Off we go.

You give your horse a kick and tell it to get going. Nothing happens. It appears to have dozed off. How embarrassing.

You do a lot more kicking, flap the reins about and shout. A few people stop what they are doing to watch you, but the horse takes no notice whatever, the idle and pig-headed brute.

You have just used up a lot of energy and it has all been wasted. The reason it has been wasted is that when you flap about wildly with your arms and legs your energy is going into the atmosphere and not into the horse.

Let's pretend that didn't happen and start again.

Keep calm and before you do anything else, THINK. Think

about how you are going to get the horse to move forward; work it out in your mind. Concentrate.

Now, take a deep breath so you make yourself as light as possible, then sit down and feel your weight going down into the saddle. The horse will feel that weight acting directly on his spine – you are saying 'Listen to me. I'm talking to you.'

Then, use your legs. Bring your lower legs into contact with the sides of the horse and squeeze. It's like a vice, with all your energy flowing inwards, into the horse.

That squeeze is the signal for the horse to move. The power that propels the horse forward comes from the hindquarters (back legs) so by squeezing with your legs it is as if you were turning on the engine – and the horse moves forward. As it moves, relax your legs and give slightly with the reins so that your hands follow the movements of the horse's head.

Success. Take back that bit about the idle and pig-headed brute.

It would be silly to pretend that every riding-school horse is going to cooperate every time. But the more positive you can be – leaving no doubt in your own mind about what you want to do, and as far as possible no doubt in the horse's mind – the more chance you have of success.

'The school' is a large area either indoors or outside where a group of people can be given a lesson in the charge of one instructor. You ride round and round the track in circles but whichever way you are going the side nearest the wall is your outside and the side nearest the middle the inside. If you are turning right, you are on the right track, turning left, left track.

Bringing off a really perfect turn on a horse takes a lot of practice, but for a start, if you want to turn left, close your fingers round the left rein and move your right leg back just behind the girth. If you want to turn right, squeeze the right rein and move your left leg back.

The point of moving the outside leg back is that when you get more experienced you use it to control the horse's hindquarters, so that they do not swing round too much on the turn. The inside leg stays on the girth maintaining the horse's forward movement (impulsion) and giving it just that little bit more for the turn.

To turn a horse you only have to squeeze one rein gently. All beginners tend to try to pull the horse's head round much too far (natural instinct getting it wrong again). When you do it properly the horse should turn its head just enough for you to be able to see its eyelashes as it goes round the corner.

After a while the aids for turning become automatic and you can stop trying to remember which is your left hand or your right leg. If you get in a muddle at the beginning, don't worry — no horse is stupid enough to run smack into the wall of an indoor school.

Increasing speed is a matter of using your legs again. 'LEGS, LEGS, LEGS,' the instructors shout when they want you to get from walk to trot or from trot to canter. And that means that you have to squeeze or kick with your lower legs to get the horse to speed up. If you are riding a lazy horse you will find that you have to use your lower legs quite a lot just to keep it going at the speed you want.

It takes time for your leg aids to become effective because it is the muscles on the insides of your legs that you are using, muscles that you do not normally use, so you have to bring them to life gradually. The more you ride, the stronger they will become. Don't worry, it is just a matter of time.

Using your legs effectively from the knee down depends on how well you are balanced from the knee up. Without a good deep seat in the saddle you are going to get the wobbles every time you have to kick on.

Once you have used your legs to increase the speed, make sure you are ready for the change of pace. You have asked for it so it should not come as a surprise to you. THINK about it before it comes; get balanced and into position as it happens.

All the aids to trot, canter and gallop are textbook stuff, but before you do anything else, think. Get the thought of what you are going to do fixed in your mind and then follow through with your back, seat, legs and hands. If you want to get from trot to canter, THINK canter, sit down in the saddle, bring one leg slightly back behind the girth and squeeze with both legs. Then, as the horse responds, give with your hands, because at canter the horse needs to move its head backwards and forwards freely as it moves.

(Remember that to get a horse into canter you must start from a sitting trot. No well-schooled horse will ever canter while you are in a fast trot. It will just keep trotting round no matter what you do.)

Just a word about canter. Before you try it, all your horse-riding friends will be telling you how easy it is and how much you are going to enjoy it.

'Just like sitting in an armchair,' they say. 'Wonderful sensation.'

Oh yes?

Well, it is a wonderful sensation, but it is not like sitting in an armchair.

I longed to canter. Couldn't wait. So they said I could try it. We went round the corner (sitting trot), then squeeze with both legs – and CAN-ter. My first thought was that the horse I was riding must be physically deformed. Not only were we going up and down but we were going round and round as well. And all this while flying across the school at a truly incredible pace.

I wanted to go home – and so did the horse, who made straight for the gate. Fortunately the gate was shut.

Having got me back and straightened their faces, the know-alls explained that the canter was a circular motion and that going round and round was quite normal. 'Rather like being on a wave,' they said. 'As it rolls, you must let yourself roll with it.' Thank you very much. After that we tried it again and this time it was better.

The trouble with people who have been riding for years is that it is almost impossible for them to imagine what it is like for a beginner.

Once you have got the hang of it, the canter becomes the high point of the lesson – that is, until you start learning to jump.

Apart from thinking all the time, the other general rule is to ride actively. People who complain that the horse they have been given to ride 'won't trot' or 'won't canter' are giving themselves away. The instructors know that there is nothing wrong with the horse – it is the people who are lazy. If the rider is not willing to work, why should the horse bother?

Riding actively does not mean lunging about in the saddle and waving your elbows. It does not do any good and it looks awfully silly. More like rowing a boat than riding a horse.

How do you stop a horse? You stop it by sitting down in the saddle like a dead weight (the opposite of riding actively). You wish to stop, you are thinking stop and you are not cooperating with any forward movement. Then squeeze with both legs and resist with your hands. Don't pull. That's asking for trouble. If you get involved in a tug of war with a horse you will lose because the horse is a lot stronger than you are. Just resist, close your hands round the reins, squeeze with your legs, brace your back (as if you were sitting on a stool and tipping it forward) and then keep still.

If the horse does not stop the first time you ask, try again. There really is nothing to worry about, so keep calm and go through the whole process again.

People learning to ride probably worry more about not being able to stop their horses than anything else. There again, if you are learning to ride under supervision at a properly run school, you have the reassurance of knowing that your horse will not go far because the instructors will not let it.

Once you get more experienced and are allowed to ride outside the school, the same problem may occur again. The sight of all that open space can make a new rider nervous. If you do let your nerves get the better of you, your horse *might* take the opportunity to go a bit further or a bit faster than you had in mind.

What do you do if that happens?

Well, by then you should know enough to get into position, get balanced and prepare yourself to take control and pull up.

Never mind the horse: it's your own feelings you have to master first – you *are going to keep calm*; and you *are going* to take charge of the situation. Don't waste time calling for help – it really is up to you. The horse is not a homicidal lunatic; it has not had a brainstorm, it is just playing games. Having got that straight in your mind, the process of stopping becomes much easier. You can start by steering it round in a big circle so that you are not too far away from where you want to be.

There's a lot of nonsense talked about horses 'bolting'. A trained riding school horse would have to be very frightened indeed to really, truly bolt. But all non-riders have their stories about bolting horses: 'I've only been on a horse once in my life and it bolted.' No it didn't. It just put a bit of speed on and you panicked.

THE REINS

The experts will tell you that people are either born with 'good hands' or they are not. 'Good hands' means that you have the right sort of touch on the reins – light, responsive and sensitive. It may be true that some people are born with good hands, but whatever you are born with you can improve on nature.

The reins are the most subtle of all the ways in which you can communicate with your horse. When you take up the reins you begin a conversation with your horse that will last until you get off. Taking up the reins, you make contact with the horse's mouth – 'Hello, I'm here. This is your captain speaking.'

To move forward you squeeze with your legs and as the horse walks forward you allow your hands to follow the movements of the horse's head (just a slight movement, not too much).

The reins are held between the thumb and first finger of each hand, thumb on top, pressed down firmly, to stop them slipping. Then you curl your fingers round the reins, pointing inwards so that you can see your finger nails. The reins go between your fourth and your little finger – again to stop them slipping through your hands.

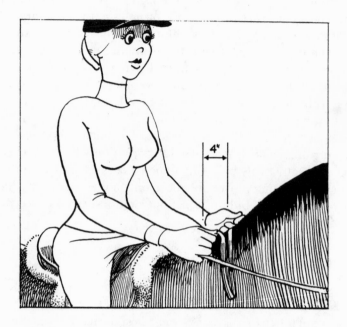

Your upper arms should be completely relaxed and your elbows close to your sides. There should be a straight line from your elbows to your hands, through the reins to the horse's mouth.

Keep your hands fairly low – on an average riding-school horse about one or two inches above the withers should be about right. Your hands should be about four inches apart – or roughly the same width as the bit. So you have the bit on one end going through the horse's mouth and your hands at the other. If you think of the bit as being rather like a dentist's drill, you will understand why your hands need to be light and sensitive.

Through the reins you let the horse know what you want to do, not force it to obey you through pain.

When you first start learning to ride it is difficult to know how much you need to do with the reins to get a horse to turn or to stop. Can it really be true that you only need to squeeze your fingers round the rein? The instructor tells you to turn left and before you know it your left hand has shot two feet out to the side.

'Wrong,' they say. 'Keep your hands still. Just close your fingers round the rein. Squeeze it like a sponge.'

As you squeeze you are shortening the rein very slightly on one side and since the reins are not made of elastic the only thing that can give is the side of the horse's mouth. The horse feels the pressure and knows what you want. Once you have let the horse know what you want and the horse has responded, relax the pressure.

The communication between horse and rider through the reins is a means of mutual reassurance. Do not underestimate yourself. The horse likes to know you are there and that you are in control. If you ride with the reins too long, the contact will be broken and when you do want to use them there will be a jerk – it's like putting down the telephone during a conversation and then coming back and shouting into it.

When you want to stop a horse you squeeze the reins with both hands – restraining the forward movement. Combined with the back and leg aids this is quite enough.

If you want to convince yourself that squeezing the reins is all that is needed, try experimenting with a chair. Tie two pieces of string to either side of the back of a chair and hold the ends as you would hold the reins. Then squeeze with both hands and the chair will tip backwards towards you. If you squeeze with only one hand as you would for a turn, the chair will tip backwards on one side.

Keeping the reins at the right length and maintaining a steady contact with the bit without pulling only comes with practice. As a beginner you may think that you are getting it right, but your horse knows better. You may be trotting along without a care in the world when you get a sudden, violent tug on the reins from the horse. Jerked rudely out of your daydream you may feel a sense of injustice. What on earth did the stupid animal do that for?

Unfortunately, your horse *knows* the minute you allow your attention to wander, and he does not like it. You have to concentrate all the time when you are riding and you need to be totally absorbed in what you are doing.

That is one of the pleasures of riding; it is a rare chance to block out everything else and devote yourself to the enjoyment of the moment. Nothing matters but you and your horse and the business of getting to understand one another.

THREE

Getting It Together

The aids are all designed to work together, and it is the rider's job to coordinate them. If you are 'pushing on' with your legs, asking the horse to move forward, but you have forgotten about your hands and are still holding back with the reins, what is the horse supposed to do?

He will think you are an idiot.

Let the aids flow smoothly, one into another. First the thought – make up your mind, then, like a current of electricity, the signals pass down through your back, seat and legs, into your hands and from you into the horse. If you want to move forward, ask for that forward movement with your back and legs and then release it with your hands – ride *from* your legs *into* your hands. It is like bending a twig and then releasing one end – the free end will spring away.

Riding is a series of messages from the rider to the horse and from the horse back to the rider.

Suppose you want to turn right. You apply the aids, saying 'turn right'. The horse starts to turn – 'O.K. I'm turning.' You relax the aids – 'That's fine. That's what I wanted.'

There is no reason why you should not actually talk to your horse. It is one of the accepted aids and will help to make you and the horse feel more relaxed. Notice how the instructors use their voices to control the horses during the

41

lesson and the horses understand exactly what they mean. Apart from competitors in dressage competitions (and we are not quite ready for that yet) you will see people talking to their horses all the time. Use your voice when you want to, to supplement the other aids.

Occasionally you may have to use a whip or a stick. If you are quite sure that the horse understands what you want but he just will not do it, a quick tap with a whip is much better in the end than a lot of violent kicking, which is quite likely to upset your balance. Using the whip in this way you are using it as an aid and not as a punishment. Your whip should support your leg, and if you need to use it, use it behind the leg.

When you first begin to ride, just thinking about your position and balance and wondering whether you are going to fall off takes up your whole attention. Then, when you find that you don't fall off, you have time to think about what is happening underneath you, what the horse is doing.

You have been getting used to the movements of the horse at walk, trot and canter. The sensations for the rider are different because the horse puts his feet down in a different sequence at different paces.

When a horse walks he just puts one foot down after another. At the trot a horse lifts two feet off the ground simultaneously – the ones in opposite corners (or 'the diagonals'). Then, before those two feet hit the ground again he lifts the other diagonals off. You hear two hoof beats.

Rising to the trot you can choose which pair of diagonals you rise on. A left diagonal would be the left foreleg and the right hindleg; a right diagonal the right foreleg and left hindleg. If you choose to rise on a left diagonal, watch the horse's left shoulder. It will move towards you while the left foreleg is on the ground – that's when you should be sitting. As the horse lifts its left foreleg, you rise. When you are rising to the trot for any length of time it is less tiring for the horse if you change diagonals every so often.

At canter you hear three hoof beats. First the horse puts

down one of its hind feet (one beat), then the other hind foot and the diagonal front foot together (two beats) and then the last front foot (three beats). The horse is doing a right lead canter if its right foreleg is leading and a left lead canter if its left foreleg is leading (that is the foreleg that comes down last – on the third beat).

'Which lead are you on?' they ask brightly as you canter down the school. They mean the horse, of course, not you.

How should I know?

'Well, take a look and see.'

You take a look and find out which of the horse's front legs is coming down last and leading (moving ahead of the other one). If it is the right leg you are said to be on the right lead, and vice versa.

Whichever way you are going you will almost certainly find that the horse is leading with the leg nearest the centre of the school – away from the wall. Cantering round the track, it is much easier for the horse to keep its balance if the inside leg is leading – otherwise it might get its front legs tangled up going round the corner. The instructors make sure that this does not happen.

You can get a horse to lead with its right or left front leg by making sure it strikes off into canter with the opposite hind leg.

When you think about it, the aid to canter is always taught in a school as being to bring your *outside* leg (the one nearest the wall) back behind the girth. What you are really doing is giving the horse a dig in the ribs (or, more correctly an upward nudge) with your leg, saying 'strike off with *that* leg'. If the horse strikes off with its outside hind leg the inside foreleg will be leading.

The more you know about what the horse is doing, the easier it is to respond and to anticipate the next move. Your lessons will give you an opportunity to ride different horses and you will find that some of them move more smoothly than others, some are lazy and some are nervous. Sometimes you may be having a bad day, and sometimes the horse you are riding may be having a bad day and sometimes everything may go like a dream. You have to allow for these things.

Your use of the aids has to be adapted to suit each horse. A lazy horse will need stronger use of the aids. Always start by using them gently, then if nothing happens, increase the pressure. Very roughly the classier the horse the more he is likely to respond to the most delicate use of the aids.

Horses like people who know their own minds. Once you have decided what you want, once you have made that mental

44

commitment, you have to be willing to see it through no matter how much time it takes, or patience. Never, never lose your temper. Self-control is important in all sports, but in riding it is a basic requirement. To control a horse you need to keep a clear head, and you need to keep calm. Whether you like it or not, your body is going to transmit your feelings to the horse.

For a horse, carrying a rider who is frightened is like trying to concentrate while someone in the same room is running up and down shouting fire. For their size, horses are surprisingly nervous animals. It is up to you to supply enough quiet confidence for two. It is your job to reassure the horse – not the other way round. You must make him feel that while he is with you he is safe.

Most horses want to please, so it is important, when your horse has done something well, to give him plenty of praise and show that you appreciate his efforts. If you can make it clear that you know when he is trying his best and that you are pleased with him, he is much more likely to go well for you. We all like a bit of encouragement when we are trying hard and horses are no different.

All this is inevitably bringing you into some sort of relationship with your horse. During the course of one lesson your feelings towards your horse will vary. One minute you are cursing him under your breath, and then if you think canter, ask for canter and get canter, he is just the best horse in the world.

But no matter how things work out during the lesson, the moment you dismount and your feet touch the ground is the moment you are going to feel most affection for that animal. There is something about that moment that is pure magic. (It could be relief and gratitude that you are still in one piece, couldn't it?) Anyway it is a very moving experience.

Watch people at the end of a ride. Shining faces, big smiles, lots of patting and fussing the horses.

But what about the horses? Not a lot going on there as far as you can tell. At the end of a ride you may be surrounded by

45

horses. They all have names and you can tell one from another, but what are they really like?

FOUR

Getting to Know Horses

If you ask people to generalise about horses they generally talk rubbish. 'Horses are not intelligent,' they say. They then go on to tell you about some of the horses they have known who have been very intelligent, blessed with enough intuition and wit to make the mind wilt, by all acounts.

So horses are not intelligent – except for some of them – who are intelligent.

Press on.

They tell you that horses cannot reason but they have very good memories. Horses remember what they have been taught and they also remember any unhappy experiences they may have had. Very few horses are born vicious, but if they have been mistreated, they can be difficult. It is never the horse's fault.

Quite. How can they be difficult?

'Well, take Hector.'

What about Hector?

Hector, it seems, was bought about five years ago, arrived in a trailer and was put into a box stall without giving any trouble at all. What no one knew was that Hector had been half starved when he was young. When a stable girl went into his box with his food, Hector picked her up in his teeth and threw her straight out into the yard over the stable door.

'He didn't like anybody coming near him when he was

eating, you see.'

Yes, I can see that.

Some horses seem to respond to one person more than to others, but they are usually most fond of the people they see every day, who feed them, groom them and clean out their boxes. You have to spend a lot of time with them before you really get to know them.

'Like poor old Nutmeg.'

Here we go again. What happened to Nutmeg?

Nutmeg was a dear old thing who had the habit of pulling terrible faces. She wouldn't have hurt anyone for the world; she just liked pulling faces to see if anyone was impressed. At one time she was sent to another stable for a while where the staff did not know what to expect. They took her seriously and started going into her box in twos and threes armed with brooms to protect themselves.

Poor old Nutmeg was nearly frightened out of her wits. When the time came to collect her she was led out of the box on a double lunge with two people hanging on to each end. Her owner took one look at them all and told them to let go.

As soon as she was free, Nutmeg walked over to her owner and then hurried into the trailer. She was obviously very relieved to be getting out of that madhouse and going home.

Poor old Nutmeg.

If you are learning to ride, you presumably like horses and hope you have some sort of empathy with them. For a start you can walk round the stable yard and talk to them.

Some horses like physical affection and some do not. It is unfortunate that a horse looking out of its box sticks out nose first. Remember that because a horse's eyes are set on the sides of its head, it can't get you into focus if you stand directly in front of it. We've all been brought up on the idea that horses like to be patted on the nose. People would not like it if they were patted on the nose and quite a few horses do not like it either.

Never patronise a pony. If they are small they may look very sweet but it does not mean they feel sweet. They may regard themselves as fully grown and serious animals. Once you get to know a pony you can be as affectionate as you like, but have some respect for their feelings.

Walking round the stables it would be nice to have a life history of each horse tacked up outside the stable door to tell you all about them. All horses are different, but what is it about their character and personality that makes one horse different from another?

Here are a few examples of the completely individual horses kept at one riding school, described by the person who knows them best – their owner:

This is Charley. He's a 14.2 hands brown Cob gelding and he's twenty years old.

Charley was given to the school when his owner decided she was too old to ride him – she was seventy-five. He had been trained by her to keep to a walk or a trot because if he went any faster she thought she might fall off. It took us three weeks to get him to canter – we had to try everything. He just couldn't believe that he was allowed to go that fast. He still moves at a nice sedate pace, though.

He doesn't particularly like being fussed over, but he will follow you anywhere for a peppermint.

He's ideal for beginners – a real 'schoolmaster' who takes care of his rider and shows them how it should be done. And he responds to the instructor's voice instantly.

This is Lady Jane. She's 15.2 hands. A grey Hunter mare. She's perfect for anyone from a child to a much older novice rider. She will walk, trot, canter and jump, but if the rider loses their balance the instructor only has to shout 'stop' and she stops. At the same time she has plenty of go and will give anyone an enjoyable ride up to the standard they are capable of maintaining.

She's an introvert. Very shy. If you creep up quietly and kiss her on the nose she will run to the end of her box and hide for at least ten minutes. She loves to please, though. Most horses have large, brown eyes, but you can tell from the expression in her eyes that she's a nice horse. She listens to every word you say. You can see her ears following you because she is interested.

Horses are very nosy creatures. If there is something going on in the yard they will practically break their necks trying to see what is happening.

This is Jason. He's 14.2 hands; a gelding, ten years old. He's every beginner's delight because of his quiet nature. He gives them confidence. With an expert on his back he is capable of plenty of speed and of tackling any obstacle, but he prefers to wander through the countryside chewing a bit of straw with a complete novice on his back. He hates exercise really.

Once you have mastered the art of sitting and riding correctly – once he knows you mean it, he will do it. But his excuse is always 'I can't do that because they might fall off'.

This is Prince. A black Dartmoor pony. 12.1 hands; thirteen years old; a gelding.

He's the perfect riding child's pony. In the stable he is aggressive and inclined to bite – he's 12.1 but thinks 16.2.

Once saddled and bridled there's a complete change of personality and he comes into his own. He's a gem.

There was one time when a child was riding him and jumping; just as they were going over the jump the child fell off. Prince was in mid air. He got his front feet down but if he had brought his hind legs down he couldn't have avoided the child who was lying on the ground just in front of him, so he bellyflopped onto the jump and stayed there, rocking, until we dashed up, dragged the child away and rescued him.

No horse will tread on you if he can possibly avoid it.

This is Dainty. A 13 hands piebald mare. Thirteen years old. She's a perfect leadline pony. Quite all right on a leadline or on a carefully supervised hack, but a handful for a medium to competent rider on their own.

50

She's a pony with a sense of humour. Her idea of a joke is to stand still in one corner of the school until you wallop her, then she gallops across the school and stands still in the opposite corner.

And this is her daughter – Pandy. Eight years old; a 13.2 hands piebald mare.

Pandy is completely neurotic about her mother and hates being parted from her. If Dainty is in sight, Pandy will rush across and get as close to her as she possibly can – not that Dainty is all that pleased to see her!

With Dainty out of the way, Pandy is the perfect children's pony. She's capable of doing everything from taking a complete novice to enjoying a day's hunting.

This is Brownie. A thoroughbred gelding. 16 hands. He's six.

Brownie is not a beginner's ride. He's strong and quick on the uptake, but he still has a lot to learn. He's very interested in his surroundings and quite all right at walking and trotting, although he is a bit bouncy, but having lulled his rider into a false sense of security, when they ask for canter, he explodes into action. He's not trying to put them on the floor – it's just his way of expressing his high spirits.

He loves human companionship. He likes standing with his head out of his box and anything up to twelve children all patting him and pulling his ears. As long as he's getting a lot of attention, he's happy.

If there is no one about to talk to him, he likes watching the cows in the next field. They're great friends of his and he spends hours staring at them. One time we started parking the horse trailer opposite his box and he got very moody. We couldn't think what was the matter with him and then we realised that we were blocking his view – he couldn't see his cows any more. As soon as we moved it he was all right again.

This is Billy. 16 hands. A bay Irish horse, five years old.

Poor old Billy is completely unable to look after himself, so you have to do the thinking for him. He's not a beginner's ride.

He's got liquid eyes that look trustfully out on the world. He truly believes that you know best even if you are doing something really stupid.

Everyone loves Billy. He's a genuinely affectionate horse. Because he's young he sometimes seems dim, but it's just that he lacks experience and he can't understand what you want. He *wants* to understand and he worries a lot. Sometimes he worries so much that he gives himself tummy ache.

He's a hypochondriac.

It's hard work in the stables, all day, every day, so spectators are not always welcome. If you want to stay long, offer to help.

You will probably be asked to sweep out the barn. It sounds straightforward, but it isn't. English stables have a reputation for being well kept and tidy and every stable owner has their own idea about how this should be done. Before you start it is just as well to find out which brush they would like you to use and in which direction they would like you to sweep. Look out for the drains. Stable owners react violently to people who block up their drains with bits of hay and straw.

Having succeeded in sweeping out the barn to everyone's satisfaction, you may be allowed to take the next step up the stable-management ladder and water the horses. Every horse has to have a constant supply of fresh water. About eight gallons a day for each horse in a *clean* drinking bucket.

You have to go into the box or stall, get the bucket, clean it out and fill it up.

'Move over there, Huckleberry, I'm coming in.' A horse in a stall doesn't leave you much room to get past. And it's dark in there.

'Where's the wretched bucket?'

If you can't find the bucket it means you have gone in on the wrong side. You have a choice between coming out and starting again or crawling across the floor under the horse's front feet.

Come out and start again.

'Move over there, Huckleberry'

Every horse is treated as an individual when it comes to feeding. The food is weighed out and varied according to the size of the horse and the work it is doing; keeping a balance between hay, hard food (bran, oats, nuts etc.) and succulents.

Providing for the needs of each horse takes expert knowledge, so let the experts get on with it. If they need any help, you can make yourself useful by delivering the food and hay to each horse in turn.

Get somebody to show you how to tie up the hay nets properly; they must be secure and at the right height for the horse – if they are too low the horse might get one of its feet tangled up in the net and injure itself.

You will soon find out which of the horses in the stable are the greedy ones. From the moment the first rattle of a bucket signals feeding time they will be banging on their stable doors, shaking their tins and shouting their heads off.

After a while, you may be asked to help with tacking up. Watch the experts doing it before you try it yourself. And then get them to watch you do it to make sure you are doing it correctly. If the horses stand quietly while you are tacking up it makes the job much easier. But remember that a horse will only stand quietly for you if it has been gently and expertly handled. One bit of clumsiness from a beginner who is not quite sure what they are doing could upset years of work.

While you are learning the right way to tack up, you will have the chance to get to know what all the various pieces of tack are called and what they are all for. It is not essential for anyone learning to ride to know about the tack but if you are among people who toss off a lot of technical talk about 'throat latches', 'billet straps' and 'running or standing martingales' it's nice to know what they're talking about.

Hauling bales of hay and straw about is hard work. Grooming is hard work. Cleaning out and bedding down is hard work. Cleaning the tack is hard work. If you can make yourself useful around the stables it is an energetic but enjoyable way of filling in your spare time.

And you have the chance of getting to know the horses. Next time you are in the saddle you will know more about the horse you are riding, and because you know more about your horse you will get better results.

Learning the technique of riding is not enough for good horsemanship. The key to success is sympathy with your horse and an understanding of its mentality.

FURTHER READING

Carol Green, *Tack Explained* (Arco).

FIVE

Making Progress

You are making progress. You know you are making progress because sometimes when you get the aids right the horse responds to you rather than to the instructor. Life is more interesting for you and for the horse.

There are one or two problems still outstanding though. One is staying in the correct riding position. Steering a horse round the school and changing pace it is difficult to be sure that your seat, back, legs, hands, heels and head are all where they ought to be. As soon as you get one thing right something else seems to go wrong. Everyone has the same problem, which is why the instructors always seem to be saying the same things:

'HEELS DOWN.'

'HANDS DOWN.'

'GET YOUR LEGS BACK.'

She can't mean me, surely.

'IF YOU DON'T SIT PROPERLY YOU CAN FORGET EVERYTHING ELSE. YOUR LEGS CAN'T HOLD YOU ON A HORSE. NO WAY. SIT UP, SHOULDERS BACK AND DOWN, LEGS NICE AND LONG. *BACK AND SEAT.* SIT STILL. SMALL OF SPINE RELAXED, SEAT TUCKED UNDERNEATH YOU HOLDING YOU FIRMLY IN THE SADDLE. YOUR HIPS MOVE *WITH* THE HORSE. . . .'

Yes, I know, I know, I *know*!

The trouble is that the instructors can see what you are doing and you can't.

'Turn your toes in,' they say.

You had no idea that your toes were turned out. And if they weren't does it matter? Yes, it does matter because if you turn your toes out two things happen:

1. Your knees come away from the sides of the saddle, your seat is pushed back, you lose your balance and you may fall off.
2. If your toes are pointing out your heels kick the horse in the ribs at every stride. The horse thinks that means you are in a hurry and he goes faster and faster.

The real secret of riding that is not always explained as clearly as it might be is that when it comes down to it, it is all a matter of common sense.

The 'correct riding position' is not just aesthetically pleasing for the onlooker, it is the only possible way to sit on a horse – and stay there.

As you get better and become more relaxed you learn to use your own weight to keep you firmly in the saddle and your balance improves. With practice your leg muscles get more supple so your leg closes round the horse and when you want to use your leg aids all you have to do is squeeze and relax. That long-term goal of an independent seat is getting nearer.

There will be talk, at this stage, about how to get your horse balanced. For a comparative beginner, balancing horses sounds rather advanced stuff. You have a sudden, awful vision of the damn thing keeling over if you do something wrong.

Don't worry about it.

At walk, trot and canter just ride the horse as you have been taught to ride it and follow any transitions in pace as smoothly as you can.

At this stage the best way to keep your horse balanced is to concentrate on your own balance. As long as you are balanced, relaxed and following the movements of your horse you should not have to do anything else *at this stage* to correct the horse.

A balanced horse simply means that the horse is carrying

itself in the right way. If you were riding a young horse who had not been properly schooled you would have problems, but a riding school horse knows what it is doing.

In their natural state horses carry most of their weight on their forehand (front legs). When they are schooled they are taught to distribute their weight more evenly over all four feet; to bring their hind legs well underneath them, to round their backs and to carry their heads higher than they would naturally. From head to tail their bodies are as short as possible and being compressed like that means that the horse can make the best possible use of its hindquarters – where the power comes from. If you look at photographs of horses taking part in dressage competitions, you can see that wonderful rounded shape of the hindquarters, back and neck. You can see the power in the hindquarters ready to drive the horse forward.

Instructors may ask you to 'collect' your horse – they mean that they want you to bring both ends underneath you – get it together. A collected horse is an effective horse. Once the horse is the right shape, the rider controls the driving force of the hindquarters with his back, seat and legs and then he releases that power through his hands. It's like a coiled spring. When you release one end with your hands, you're away!

Getting back to your own balance, the riding position you have been taught is the best one for flat work and dressage. It is also the best position for a beginner because with your legs long it is easier to stay on and easier to control the horse. You are balanced between those two straight lines – one from your hands to your knee to your toe; one from the back of your head to your seat to your heel. All you have to do is stay there – as no doubt you have been told until you are sick of hearing it. But what happens when you want to gallop or when you want to jump?

If you want to gallop or jump you are going to have to lean forward. And in your present riding position if you lean forward you would be in danger of falling off.

So you have to increase your area of balance to allow for

The power comes from the hindquarters

leaning forward.

You do that by shortening your stirrups. With shorter stir-rups your legs are bent up underneath your body. So from the back of your seat to your knee there is much more room.

That is your new area of balance. It's wider, so now you can safely lean forward when you want to.

Because riding is all about common sense, when somebody gets it right it *looks* right, and when somebody gets it wrong it looks terrible. Building up a mental picture of how it should look is the first step. The difficulty is that you can't watch your-self. Looking at other riders during the lesson, you can see that something seems to be going wrong, but it is not always easy to identify exactly where they are making the mistake. The in-structors know. They can see both cause and effect and it is their job to put things right before cause and effect result in dis-aster.

Riding instructors do tend to express themselves forceably and loudly when they are giving a lesson. Don't be put off by this. Don't be depressed if you make a mistake and the instruc-tor makes it sound as if it is the first time anybody has ever done anything so silly on a horse. They have seen it all before a thousand times, which is why they are so fluent. Everybody makes mistakes, and since you are there to learn you must expect criticism. A good instructor will make sure that you get some encouragement as well as a vivid account of your short-comings, but the criticism should be given – and taken – with good humour. It is worth recording a few typical riding instruc-tors' tirades because they contain a good deal of information in concentrated form. So, leaving out the jokes and the more colourful language, here they are:

First Mistake: Turning badly

INSTRUCTOR: 'This time as you come down the school I want you to turn at B marker . . .'
(The rider comes down the school and turns at B marker)

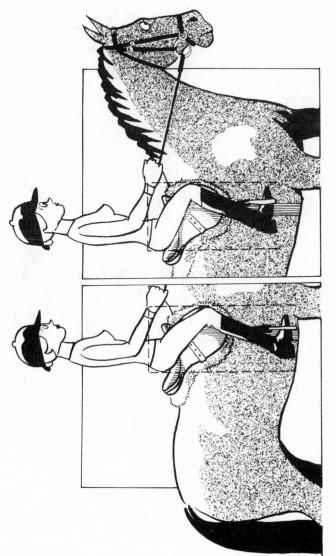

Increasing your area of balance

INSTRUCTOR: 'That was TERRIBLE. When I ask you to turn I don't mean leave it to the last minute and yank and kick. If you had been doing it properly, THINKING, you would have made sure you were prepared, wouldn't you?

As you approach the turn, think about your legs. Your inside leg is THE PIVOT ROUND WHICH THE HORSE IS GOING TO TURN. It is also the impulsion. Your outside leg controls the swing of the hindquarters. It can be either a passive or an active leg – either allowing the hindquarters to come round, or retaining them if they come round too much.

What about your reins? You relaxed the pressure on your outside rein.

If you were riding a motorbike you wouldn't let go of one side of the handlebars when you were turning a corner would you?

It's the same with the reins. Your inside rein is used for direction and bend, but your outside rein is JUST AS IMPORTANT. It must act as a support and it also controls the impulsion.

Now, do it again. And remember that as the horse turns, your shoulders follow the horse's shoulders and your hips follow the horse's hips.

Get the horse moving . . . get the engine running . . . you can't steer a stationary object, can you?

Right, trot on. . . .'

Second Mistake: Not controlling impulsion

INSTRUCTOR: 'It's all right. I've got you. Calm down. You said canter to that horse and she went tearing off round the school like a wall-of-death rider. You asked her for impulsion and she said RIGHT–WE'RE–GOING – but it wasn't quite the speed you intended.

You must control that impulsion. She wanted to go. You asked for it, but you didn't want quite as much as she was willing to give. YOU MUST USE YOUR HANDS PROPERLY. USE YOUR BACK AND SEAT. You can't stop a horse with your hands, you're not strong enough. You should use your legs to drive the horse up into the bit on to a RETAINING hand, so her own body weight and balance will pull her up. The second you start leaning forward, flapping about, she's won.

Never scream when you're on the back of a horse because the horse might start off thinking 'Oh, I'll just have a bit of a gallop round the corners. That'll shake them.' She's pretending. She's teasing. She wasn't going to go any faster and when she'd been round once she would have stopped anyway. Half way round you start screaming your head off – you have instantly told that horse HELLO, SOMETHING'S HAPPENING. You have put *your* fear into the horse and the horse starts to run away from *you*. So there you are sitting there and screaming and the horse is running away from you, and there's no end to that. . . .'

65

Third Mistake: Bad position

INSTRUCTOR: 'GET YOUR HANDS DOWN. You're jagging on the horse's mouth. He's got the bit at the back of his mouth and he's hanging on with his teeth. His head is right up in the air.

You're sitting on the back of the saddle bouncing up and down on his kidneys. He's hollowed his back to try and get away from you. He's got his head up one end and his bottom up the other and this kind of hammock effect in the middle. If you sit like that, the best behaved horse in the world will start to hollow out.

Get into position, for God's sake – if you tried to walk around like that you'd fall flat on your back. Move forward, get your seat tucked underneath you. There should be enough room behind you in the saddle to take the width of your hand. I've told you that before haven't I? You weren't listening.

Now, bend your elbows – remember that there should be a straight line from your elbows to your hands, through the reins to the horse's mouth. You knew that, did you? Well, do it then.

Your elbows must be relaxed and that means starting at the shoulders – get your shoulders relaxed and then your elbows can do their job properly – taking up the movements of your arms so that your hands don't jump up and down. A relaxed elbow gives you an independent hand. Right?

Remember all your joints are there to act as shock absorbers. At trot or canter your knees and ankles act in the same way as the springs of a car – taking up all the shocks as you move along, otherwise you would bounce yourself out of the saddle.

Now let's see you in position.

That's much better. Good. It feels better doesn't it? Yes, I imagine it would.

As a matter of fact it is more comfortable for the horse too. The way you were going on he would have been in for a nasty dose of back ache.'

Fourth Mistake: Horse not collected

INSTRUCTOR: 'That horse has got all his weight on his fore-hand. He's pulling himself along with his front feet and not using his back at all. You're sitting there in the saddle and there's this loose thing coming along behind you.

Sit up straight. Use your back and seat and PUSH the horse's hind legs underneath him. *Make* him use them.

As he brings his hind legs underneath him, use your hands.

It's not a case of pulling, it's HOLDING AND BALANCING. If you don't take up the reins properly, every ounce of effort the horse is putting into it is being wasted because it's falling straight down onto his forelegs again and going off into the ground through his nose.

You want him to round out the whole of his back from ears to tail – hind legs tucked underneath him, nice springy rounded back, neck arched, head tucked in.

That's the shape you want and that horse is quite capable of doing it. He's got muscles

68

running from his ears right down the top of his spine. It's your job to make him use them.

So as he brings his hind legs underneath him, use your hands – gently, gently, you're asking him to relax his jaw, arch his neck and bring his nose down.

Asking, asking ... that's better. Now you've got one whole horse instead of two ends.'

Fifth Mistake: Horse not straight

INSTRUCTOR: 'That horse is not straight. It's waggling about all over the place – its head is one way and its bottom the other and you're sitting there in the middle wondering what is going on. Imagine what that would be like in traffic!

You've got to remember what your legs are for – they don't just hang there doing nothing. You've got an inside leg and an outside leg – USE THEM. If your legs are active, you are active and you can keep that horse straight.'

(N.B. Keeping a horse straight is one of the most difficult things of all – the instructor knows that but she's not going to admit it.)

INSTRUCTOR: 'Think of the poor horse for a change. It's difficult for a horse to keep straight with four legs and you bouncing around in the middle of them.

WHEREVER YOU GO THE HORSE HAS TO GO.

Hasn't it ever occurred to you that every time you do a bit of wriggling the horse has to adjust his balance to *keep under you*.

It's not easy for him.

70

Remember when you were cantering round the school earlier on? I kept telling you WEIGHT ON THE OUTSIDE FOOT, didn't I?

That was because you were leaning in. When you lean in, the horse has to follow. He will come *in*, and come *in*, and come *in* because he's *trying* to get back under you.

You have to work all the time to keep your horse straight; using both hands and both legs, but most of all you must use your back and seat to drive the horse FORWARD. You won't achieve anything without impulsion.'

Riding instructors are there to put things right when they go wrong. What they are doing in their own quiet way is to stage manage each lesson so that every rider has a chance to learn something, to enjoy themselves and to stay on. If they think you are any good, they will nag you until you get better. The only time to worry is if they don't seem to have much to say. That could mean that they have decided you are beyond help and they are hoping you will take the hint and go away.

After a while you may be given a horse with a bit more 'go' in it, a bit more will-power, a bit faster on the turn. But the instructor will always make sure that the horse you are riding is within your capabilities.

Having got this far, the time has come to trust your instructor, trust your horse and to believe in yourself. If they say you can do it, *you can do it*.

Once you have been taught enough of the technical groundwork to know what you should be doing with your body, your legs and your hands, it is what is going on in your head that counts.

You need a combination of calmness, determination and optimism.

Optimism does not mean the blithe assumption that

nothing can go wrong. Riders who know their business know that anything can happen at any moment. They may appear casual but in fact they are fully aware of everything that is going on around them and of every movement their horse makes.

Optimism does mean that if you are asked to trot down the school and pop over a small cavaletti on the track, you make up your mind about how you are going to do it and then set off *expecting to succeed*.

Once you have decided what you want to do there is absolutely no excuse for being half-hearted about it. You need to be positive, as much for your horse's sake as your own.

You have to become an extension of your horse and he has to become an extension of you. You supply the judgement and your horse supplies the agility and strength.

SIX

Jumping

The fun starts when you begin to learn to jump.

The first stage of jumping is to learn to trot over poles laid flat on the ground. You should be able to get the horse through them without kicking them, so you have to get there at the right time and at the right speed, and not let the horse either stop in the middle or go through them flat out.

After that the instructors stick a small jump at the end of the poles – a cavaletti, which can be adjusted to be either 6, 12 or 18 inches off the ground.

Here we come, trotting down the trotting poles and there's this little jump at the end. We're nicely balanced, going at the right speed and aiming for the middle when the instructor shouts 'IMPULSION'.

What? I thought I was going fast enough.

'That's not the point. You have to be pushing with your back and seat, not to make the horse go faster, but to keep enough impulsion going so that the horse is ready for anything.'

Right. Sit down, steer *and* push. Now what?

'As you approach the jump you should incline your body forward from the hips – ready to *fold* for the jump. When you fold you go right down – shoulders down over the horse's mane. You must be ready for that, you must get there so you are with the horse as he jumps. If you don't, you'll get left behind and fall off backwards.'

74

Here we go again.

Trotting down the trotting poles, here comes the jump, lean forward, and

jump . . .

and everyone screams: 'FOLD. YOU DIDN'T FOLD. YOU *FOOL*. YOU LEANT BACK.'

Well, it wasn't so much that you *leant* back as that you were *thrown* back as the horse jumped. Until you have tried it there is no way of knowing the enormous amount of power involved when a big animal like a horse takes off for a jump.

The most noticeable thing about watching horses going over jumps is the way they stretch their necks out as they take off. The worst thing you can do is to snatch at the reins at the last minute. It is another of those awful reflex actions that happen at critical moments. The horse *needs* to stretch out to balance and get over the obstacle. He will not jump for somebody who constantly tries to pull his head back, or jabs him in the mouth as he is preparing to jump. He will refuse.

Use a neck strap when you are learning to jump (if they haven't got a neck strap, take hold of the horse's mane) and hold on to that instead of the reins.

As the horse takes off, your seat will leave the saddle, but if you can keep your weight on your thighs and knees you should not leave it too much. If you get into the habit of standing on your stirrup irons for jumping, sooner or later you will come off. Stay close to the saddle.

As the horse lands, he brings his head up and you fall back into the saddle with a bump.

Horses have their own ideas about how best to tackle a jump; there is a right place to take off for every jump, but your horse is much more likely to know where it is than you do. Only experience can give you an eye for it.

If you have a good horse, learn from him. He will get you out of all sorts of trouble if you will let him. Your job is to keep the impulsion going, stay balanced and, while maintaining a light contact with the reins, try to interfere with your horse's move-

ments as little as possible. Give yourself time, physically, to learn the technique of jumping, but get it right mentally from the moment you pop over your first cavaletti. It is *your determination* that will make the horse jump. Without that determination even the best-trained and most experienced horse can lose confidence in himself and fail. It is said that horses rarely refuse a jump – it is the riders who refuse.

SEVEN

Taking Your Riding Further

One of the side effects of riding horses is that however physically fit you were before you started, you will be fitter after a course of lessons. Your muscles will be firmer, your body will be more supple and you will probably have lost weight.

But much more interesting is the effect that riding has on your mental outlook. It is impossible to learn to ride well without also learning self-control. On horseback you cannot afford to lose your temper, or to get into a panic, and once you have made up your mind what you are going to do you have to be prepared to see it through. So if you were not born with the qualities of patience, calmness and determination, you are going to have to acquire them.

Of course not only able-bodied people can learn to ride. The North American Riding for the Handicapped Association now has over 100 operating centers in the U.S. and Canada. Their aim is simple – to give people a chance to ride and by doing so make it possible for them to enjoy increased health and happiness. They do not promise miracles, but there have been some remarkable results. Any disability leads to a sense of failure and frustration. For the disabled, riding lessons get off to a good start. Once in the saddle they can look down on the world of wheelchairs and helpers and on horseback they have four strong legs to carry them wherever they want to go. Mobility means freedom.

Riding a horse brings a new kind of freedom for the able-bodied too. Once you have mastered the basic techniques and learnt a little about the animal you are riding, the door to the countryside is open to you. On horseback you see far more than you could possibly hope to see on foot or in a car because a horse is accepted as part of the natural order of things. When you can ride you are free to enjoy a quiet amble through the woods or a gallop over the downs. No wonder the rich and privileged have always kept horses. Riding through the countryside is one of the greatest pleasures on earth.

Spending your time with horses brings its own rewards. Walking back to the stables with your horse after a ride, you can suddenly be aware of a feeling of well-being and contentment so extraordinary that it stays in your mind for months afterwards. What happened?

The fact is that horses make good company because they are quite willing to share with you their uncomplicated enjoyment of the pleasures of life.

You may decide to continue riding purely for your own enjoyment, or you may decide to make a career of it. Either way you go on learning – always.

It is a rare thing to be satisfied with your own performance – there is always more to achieve, but it is up to the individual rider to set his own standards. When you begin your lessons, nobody is willing to forecast how long it will take you to become a competent rider, but *very* roughly speaking, if you were only able to ride once a week, it would probably take you about a year to reach the stage when you were safe on a horse. After about a year you should have enough experience to be able to control a horse in or out of the school.

At this point, if you want to go on riding just for the enjoyment you get out of it, you can hack out when you want to; through your own stables you may be able to join a local riding club and add variety to your riding through taking part in the activities they organise. Or you can go on trekking or riding holidays in different parts of the country in the happy knowledge

79

that you now qualify as an 'experienced rider'. (An experienced rider can also be defined as someone with sufficient understanding of the art of horsemanship to have a very clear idea of their own limitations.)

If you do decide to follow a career with horses, explore either a college equine program (there are a number of colleges offering equestrian studies), or an equine career oriented school. In this latter, you can often attend as a working student, but in general paying students get more riding time. Whichever program you decide to follow, investigate carefully, ask for references, and pay the school a visit.

There are a limited number of vocational training centers for grooms throughout the states, and some equestrian centers offer courses in stable management. Again, investigate thoroughly before signing up. If you are serious about a career with horses, you would be well advised to get some sort of qualification under your belt and resign yourself to the fact that you are never going to be rich, although you will at least be leading a healthy, hard-working, outdoor life.

To spend your life competing in the higher realms of show jumping, eventing or dressage you are going to have to be either extremely rich or extremely lucky and preferably both. For a start, you will need your own horse, or horses, and to get hold of a horse who can take you to competition level you will have to spend a lot of money, or be good enough and lucky enough for somebody to lend you a horse or sponsor it for you. It is not impossible, if you are working at the right stable and show outstanding promise, that you will be given a chance to ride one of their horses, but *don't bank on it.*

Whatever you do, enjoy yourself. Horses are generous and sensitive animals. They are capable of responding to an intelligent rider; willing to do their best for you and ready to help you fulfil all your ambitions if you have the sense to work *with* them and to learn *from* them as you progress.

FURTHER READING

Alois Podhajsky, *The Complete Training of Horse and Rider* (Wilshire).
Carol Green, *Jumping Explained* (Arco).
Lt.-Colonel 'Bill' Froud, *Better Riding* (Scribner).
Alois Podhajsky, *The Art of Dressage* (Doubleday).
G. W. Freeman (ed.), *The Masters of Eventing* (Arco).
William Steinkraus, *Riding and Jumping* (Doubleday).
George H. Morris, *Hunter Seat Equitation* (Doubleday).

Not everyone can afford to buy their own horse; and even if you could afford one, you might not want to spend the time or the money involved in looking after it. Keeping a horse is not a hobby. If you had your own horse, kept it in a stable and looked after it single-handed, it would be more accurate to say that keeping the horse was your way of life and that your hobbies were eating and sleeping.

To keep a horse healthy and happy a daily routine something like this would be necessary:

    7.00am Check horse
                Water
                Quarter the horse (light grooming)
                Feed haynet
                Muck out
                Bed down
                Feed – hard feed

    9.30am Check horse
                Skip out droppings
                Feed day haynet

    12.30pm Check horse
                Skip out droppings

Feed – hard feed/haynet
Check water

4.30pm Check horse
Change water
Skip out droppings
Set fair bed

7.00pm Check horse
Check and refill water
Put up evening haynet
Skip out droppings
Feed – hard feed
Make horse comfortable for the night
Tidy up and check all doors and gates secure.

You will notice that during all that time you have not actually been riding. So add to that: a horse must have *at least* an hour's exercise every day. When you get back from a ride (*every time* you get back if you take your horse out more than once a day) you have to groom it and get the skin thoroughly clean, because if you leave dirt on a stable horse it will get skin disease. You must also check its feet and pick out any loose stones or nails. Grooming a horse should take about forty minutes to one hour if you do it properly.

After every ride you should also clean the tack – or AT THE VERY LEAST – check it and wash the bit.

So there you are – always presuming that you didn't get the horse soaking wet while you were out, or very hot, or very cold. And remembering that horses need to be shod (about once a month), their feet need to be oiled, they need to be wormed, clipped, have their manes and tails pulled, their teeth checked (by you) and if you want them to look nice for a special occasion you will quite likely have to wash them all over and plait their mane and tail.

AND ALWAYS PRESUMING THAT YOUR HORSE IS

IN THE BEST OF HEALTH.

What about keeping a horse in a field?

Fine. You need about two acres of grazing for each horse. (You can't use the same grazing non-stop all the year round because the ground has to be rested and treated to freshen and sweeten up the grass and to get rid of any worms.)

If the acreage is big enough, you don't have to exercise your horse every day, but when you do want to ride it there are two snags. The first is that you have to catch your horse. Standing in the middle of your two acres shouting 'Come to Mummy' doesn't always work. (Bribery is the answer to that problem.) The second is that if you don't ride regularly you are going to be restricted as to how far and how fast you can go when you do want to ride. A horse that has not been ridden for two or three weeks has to be toned up again gradually – like an athlete getting back into training. If you try to rush things you might break the horse down completely – break its wind, and that is the end of the poor animal.

You also have your daily duties to perform: once a day, and preferably twice, go and check the fences, check the water and check the horse. (See if you can catch it.) Make sure that there are no poisonous plants growing and that nobody has thrown any bottles, cans or rubbish into the field. Check the gates and the padlocks. Pick up the droppings or the grass will get sour.

You have to make sure your horse is getting enough to eat, especially in winter when you will have to give it hay and, if it is still losing weight, hard feed as well.

If there is not enough natural shelter you are going to have to build a shelter – and make sure it faces away from the north winds.

Before you ride your horse you will have to brush the coat, otherwise bits of dirt or clogs of hair might get pinched by the tack and make the horse sore.

Lastly, make sure your horse is not bored. By nature horses are herd animals and they don't like to be alone too much, so if you can't spend a lot of time with your horse yourself, you may have to consider arranging for it to have a companion or you may find one day that your horse has broken its way out of the field in search of company.

FURTHER READING

Carol Green, *Stable Management* (Arco).

If buying a horse still seems like a good idea, how would you go about it?

You need knowledgeable friends. They will tell you, if you didn't already know, what sort of a horse you are looking for. This will depend on your size, your experience, what you want the horse to do, where you are going to keep it, and how much money you have. Your friends may even know of a horse that would suit you. For a novice rider the best choice would be a 'schoolmaster'—an older horse who will look after its rider, and if you are an average size adult you will be looking for something in the region of 15 to 16 hands.

If your friends don't know of a horse that would suit you, you can read the advertisements and then, when you go to follow them up, take your knowledgeable friend with you.

When you read advertisements you are looking for facts. Some of the horses advertised may sound lovely, but 'great potential', 'ridden by a girl of three' or 'good looking' does not actually tell you anything. 'Great potential' is a matter of opinion; so is 'good looking' and 'ridden by a girl of three' is a load of rubbish.

The wording you are looking for is something along the lines of: 'snaffle-mouth'; 'good to shoe, catch, box, clip'; 'quiet in traffic'; 'good conformation'; '100% sound'; 'vets welcome'; 'kind temperament'.

You may not see everything you want in one advertisement, but there should be enough there in black and white to reassure you before you take any further interest.

If the advertisers are decent enough to tell you that the horse is 'nervous in traffic'; 'not entirely reliable yet'; 'makes slight noise', or 'needs experienced rider', BELIEVE THEM.

When you do go to see a horse, taking your knowledgeable friend with you, take your time and if you are interested arrange to go more than once.

Have a really good look at the horse and pay more attention to the state of its feet than to the expression on its face. Not that the face isn't important. You can tell a great deal from a horse's eyes and head: The horse should look alert and intelligent and its eyes should be large and kind.

Don't fall in love with it yet.

It is vital that your horse should be absolutely sound and you must do everything you reasonably can to make sure that the horse will behave well in and out of the stable.

Listen to what your knowledgeable friend has to say and then ask the owners to ride it for you. *Never* try a horse yourself until you have seen it ridden. If it throws its owner, that's his affair. No need to risk your neck.

If everything else seems favourable, and your knowledgeable friend is satisfied, it is time to make up your own mind whether you and that horse would get on well together. If you think you would suit one another, before you buy it, get your own vet to give the horse a thorough inspection. It must be your vet; the present owner's vet is not on your side in this transaction. It may seem expensive, but is well worth the money.

Here are some of the terms you will find in advertisements for horses, with explanations:

Greenbroke   Somebody has sat on it.
                                 Somebody has ridden it
                                 (we don't know for how long)

Well coupled   Well put together

Very typy	Typical of whatever type of horse is being advertised, 'cob', thoroughbred, Arab, etc.
'Keen' when ridden	Gets excited OR is 'freegoing'/lively.
Never hots up	Doesn't get excited
Good floating action	Moves well – doesn't plod
Daisy-cutting action	A long, low, sweeping action of the legs. No problem.
Occasionally seen to weave	Waves its head from side to side in the stall. The sign of a neurotic horse – or one who is very bored.
Slightly parrot mouthed	Upper teeth overhang the lower ones, causing possible difficulties in feeding.
Goes first or last	A horse who isn't fussy about where it goes in a group of horses.
Never 'marish'	Applied to mares. It means they don't display any of the bad qualities sometimes associated with mares – like being temperamental.
Cribs slightly	Chews anything chewable in the stall – a very bad habit because this can affect the lungs and respiratory system of the horse.

If you do decide to buy a horse you will obviously have thought out all the responsibilities you are undertaking. Even so, you cannot foresee every problem that will arise, so never be afraid to ask for advice and help when you need it. Owning a horse will bring you great rewards. Every bit of progress will be a shared pleasure and a shared triumph. After all the hard work you can stand back and see the results of your labours and your loving care in front of your eyes – a healthy and happy horse. What more could you ask?